STEM Projects in MINECRAFT™

The Unofficial Guide to
Building Railroads in
MINECRAFT™

RYAN NAGELHOUT

PowerKiDS
press.
New York

Published in 2019 by The Rosen Publishing Group, Inc.
29 East 21st Street, New York, NY 10010

First Edition

Editor: Greg Roza
Book Design: Rachel Rising
Illustrator: Matías Lapegüe

Photo Credits: Cover, pp. 1, 3, 4, 6, 8, 10, 12, 14, 16, 18, 20, 22, 23, 24 (background) Evgeniy Dzyuba/Shutterstock.com; pp. 4, 13 TTstudio/Shutterstock.com; pp. 6, 8, 10, 12, 14, 16, 18 (insert) Levent Konuk/Shutterstock.com; p. 8 Salamahin/Shutterstock.com; p.17 GLF Media/Shutterstock.com; p. 19 Denis Belitsky/Shutterstock.com; p. 22 Kovalchuk Oleksandr/Shutterstock.com.

Library of Congress Cataloging-in-Publication Data

Names: Nagelhout, Ryan, author.
Title: The unofficial guide to building railroads in Minecraft / Ryan
  Nagelhout.
Description: New York : PowerKids Press, [2019] | Series: STEM projects in
  Minecraft | Includes index.
Identifiers: LCCN 2017055778| ISBN 9781508169338 (library bound) | ISBN
  9781508169352 (pbk.) | ISBN 9781508169369 (6 pack)
Subjects: LCSH: Railroads–Computer simulation–Juvenile literature. |
  Minecraft (Game)–Juvenile literature.
Classification: LCC TF197 .N26 2019 | DDC 794.8–dc23
LC record available at https://lccn.loc.gov/2017055778

Manufactured in the United States of America

CPSIA Compliance Information: Batch #CS18PK: For Further Information contact Rosen Publishing, New York, New York at 1-800-237-9932

Contents

Where To?

Minecraft is an amazing game because it lets you do almost anything you want. If your goal is just to build a quiet farm and have enough to eat in Survival **mode**, you can do that for hours and hours. If you want to hunt monsters and build a huge castle, you can do that too!

Minecraft is a sandbox game, which means players can roam the world at will, building things and changing whatever they want. But some tools and structures can help you do other things in your own special world. If you're going to mine a lot, for example, it helps to build some railroads!

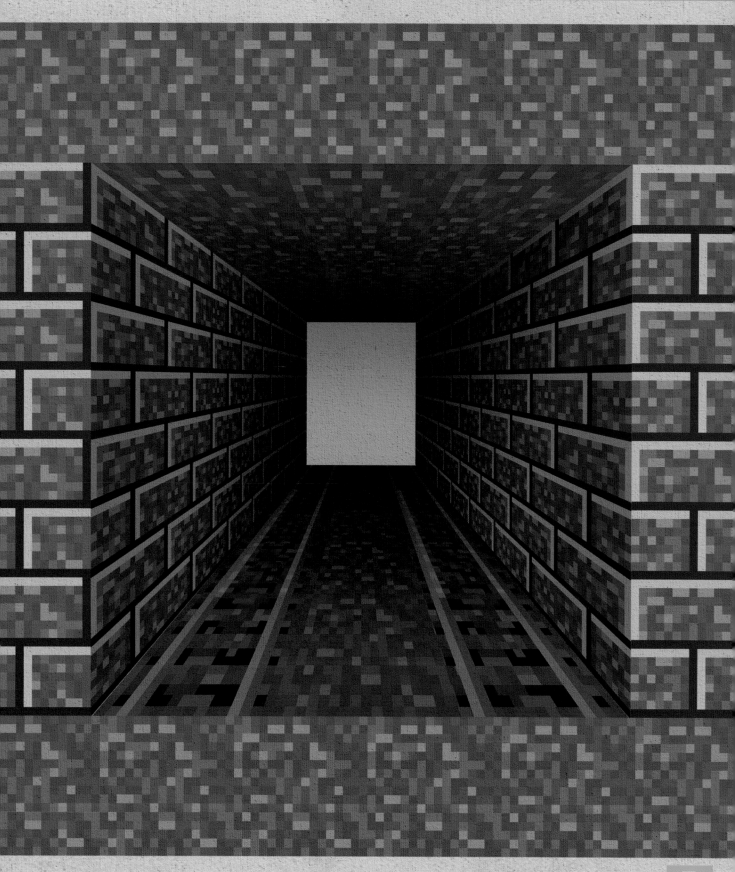

Stocking Up

Playing *Minecraft* in Creative mode is a great way to build all kinds of cool things easily and without danger. All the blocks you want to use are available right away. But if you're playing *Minecraft* in Survival mode, it will be harder to get the **resources** you need to build rails and minecarts.

You need lots of iron to build railroads. Iron is found as iron ore, which must be mined. Most iron ore is found underground and in caves. You need a lot of tools such as torches—made from sticks and coal—to go underground safely.

MINECRAFT MANIA

You need a pickaxe made of stone, iron, or diamond to mine iron ore. If you use your hand or a wooden or gold pickaxe, you won't get anything! Iron or diamond pickaxes mine iron ore faster that a stone pickaxe.

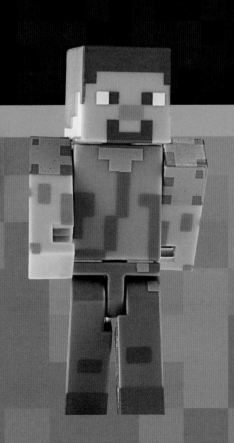

You can usually find about 77 blocks of iron ore in a **chunk** in *Minecraft*, but most iron veins are found at lower levels.

Smelt and Build

Once you find iron ore, you have to **smelt** it to make iron bricks. You need a furnace to smelt iron ore in *Minecraft*. Furnaces are made out of stone. To smelt ore, you put the ore in the furnace, then add fuel such as coal or wood. In return, you get iron bricks, also called iron ingots.

You can also make an iron ingot out of nine iron **nuggets**. It takes six iron ingots and a stick to make 16 pieces of rail for a minecart. To make a rail line that goes long distances, you need a lot of iron!

iron ingot

MINECRAFT MANIA

Rails and minecarts are made using a crafting table. You also need iron ingots to make minecarts! You need five iron ingots to make a minecart.

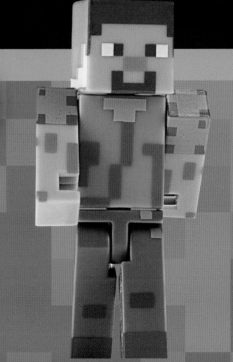

You can also find iron ingots in chests hidden in various *Minecraft* structures. They're dropped when iron golems and sometimes zombies die.

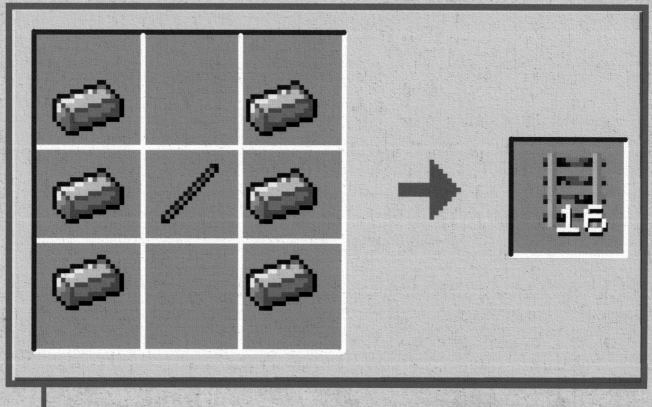

The Why and How

People build rail lines in *Minecraft* for different reasons. But most want to move themselves or other objects from one place to another. You can move much more quickly by rail than by walking. And rail lines can be built over **obstacles** such as water or lava by using bridges or through hills by digging tunnels.

Rails must be placed on solid blocks such as brick, stone, or sand. Rail lines are mostly built in straight lines, but basic rails can turn left or right. They can also go up and down one block at a time. But a minecart will need power to go up a hill!

MINECRAFT MANIA

Different *Minecraft* blocks act in different ways. Rails will be washed away if a liquid such as water or lava flows over them. Make sure you keep your rails away from water if you don't want to lose them!

Sand and gravel blocks aren't always good surfaces for rail lines because they are affected by **gravity**. If the block holding up a sand block is mined, the sand falls. This could break your rail line!

WATER

LAVA

STONE BRICKS

SAND

BRICK

Kinds of Carts

You can do many different things with rails. But the only object that moves on a rail is a minecart. There are a few different kinds. A player can hop into an empty minecart and move along a track. Other creatures can move in a minecart as well.

A minecart and chest can be combined into a minecart that stores objects. This can be used to move many things a long distance at once. Minecarts with furnaces move on their own when they're given fuel. Minecarts made with TNT will **explode** when they're touched by certain things!

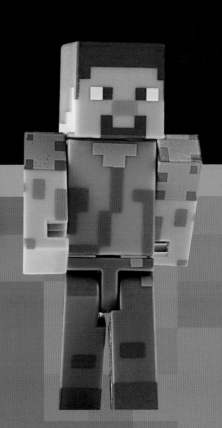

MINECRAFT MANIA

If a **mob** is pushed into a empty minecart or the minecart runs into a mob, that creature will ride in the minecart!

You can even add a hopper to a minecart. This kind of minecart will pick up items near the rail line as the cart passes by!

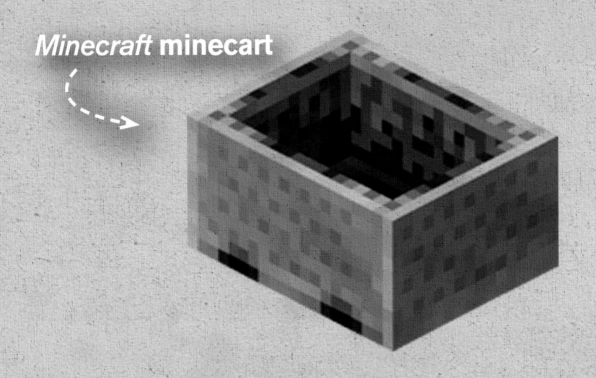

Minecraft **minecart**

real minecart

13

Making It Move

Minecarts with furnaces can move on their own, but you can also make special rails that move minecarts. Powered rails are made using six gold ingots, a stick, and a special material called redstone. This crafting recipe makes six powered rails. Gold and redstone ore can be found underground. Gold ore needs to be smelted like iron ore to make gold ingots. Redstone ore just drops pieces of redstone.

When powered rails are on, they glow! They can be activated, or turned on, by redstone torches or other power sources. Activated powered rails will move a minecart faster.

MINECRAFT MANIA

Redstone can be used to make more than powered rails. It can be used to turn rails with a **lever**, so you can control which direction a minecart travels on different sets of rails.

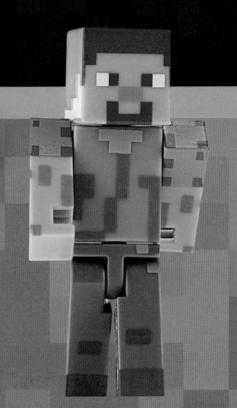

Redstone can make all kinds of cool tools that help things move. A line of redstone dust can be added between torches and other bricks to bring them to life.

15

Somewhere to Go

If you're building a real railroad, you'll need a cool building for your rail cars to stop in. At the very least, you'll want to put a block at the end of your rails so your minecarts don't leave your track! You might want to make a small station so your different kinds of minecarts go to a special place.

You have to take care of your tracks, too! You want to keep your rails well lit so mobs don't **spawn** on them. If a minecart hits something on the track, it will slow down or stop! If an empty cart hits a mob, it can pick up the mob.

MINECRAFT MANIA

Some people keep monsters or animals off their tracks by putting a wall on both sides of the rail line. That way, mobs can't stop their carts.

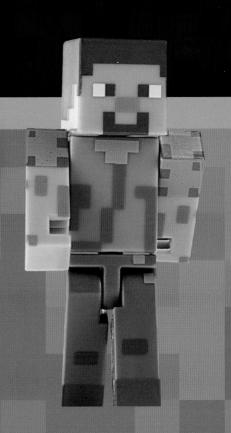

If a minecart is stopped by something, moves the other way, and hits a powered rail, the cart will start moving in the other direction!

Station to Station

You can do really cool, **complex** things with train stations if you try. Some people build secret railroads underground with secret doors they make using redstone and levers. Others make stations that look like subways you find in cities or platforms where people can wait for minecarts to come take them away.

The most useful stations in *Minecraft* help the player move things from one place to another. Most players' first rail lines will go from where resources are mined to where their home base is. This lets players mine resources quickly, then smelt them, make them into new things, or store them in chests safe from monsters!

MINECRAFT MANIA

You can make a detector rail so when a minecart drives over it, the rail detects, or senses, the cart and activates some kind of switch. These rails can be used to make all kinds of cool moving parts in *Minecraft*!

Redstone can also be used to make activator rails, which affect minecarts and can make them do different things when powered. There are lots of different things you can use them for!

Build Your Railroad Dreams!

Minecraft doesn't have real trains, just minecarts that can carry people, chests, and even TNT. But that doesn't mean you can't build big. You can use blocks to build huge train stations, even cool **art deco** stations like ones found in a big city!

You can even make your own big train out of different colored blocks, complete with passenger cars and even a caboose! And because the game doesn't have gravity, you could even put blocks in the sky above it to make it look like smoke is coming out of the engine car!

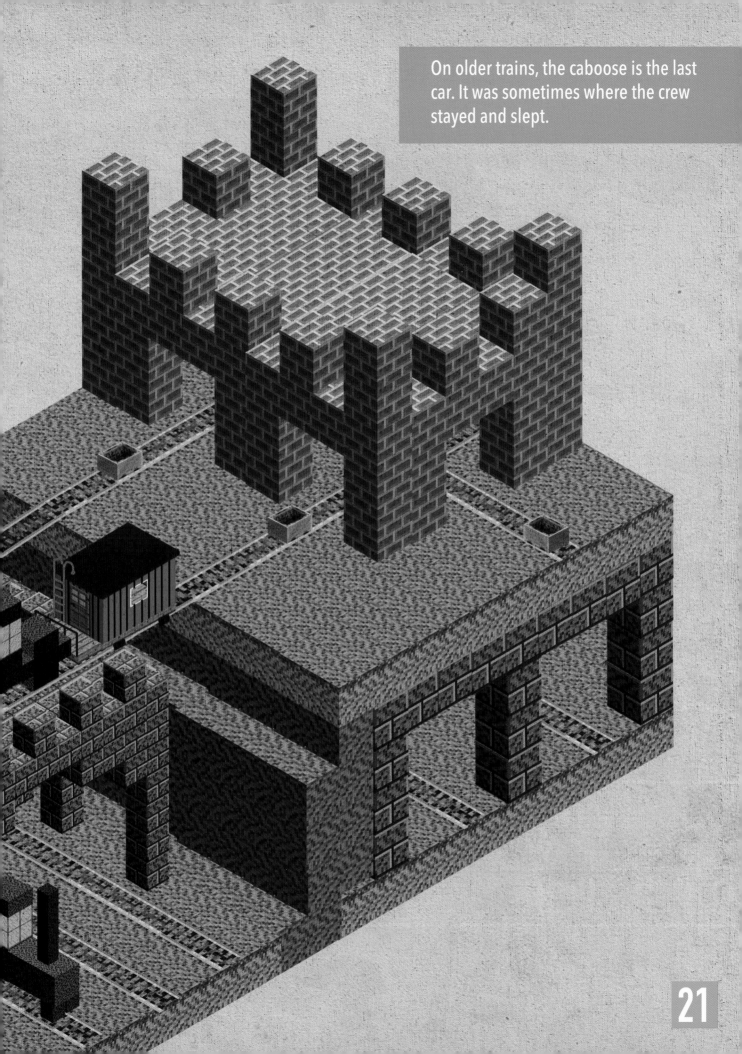

On older trains, the caboose is the last car. It was sometimes where the crew stayed and slept.

Making Mods

You can make your *Minecraft* creations even more exciting with modifications, or mods. Using a computer program called ScriptCraft, you can create new blocks, change the way the game functions, and make your own games. Imagine what you could build! You could create a railroad that crosses a volcano, or the craziest roller coaster you've ever seen!

If you're interested in learning how to create mods in *Minecraft,* visit the website below. You'll find the information needed to get started with ScriptCraft and build your own *Minecraft* mods. **https://scriptcraftjs.org**

Glossary

art deco: A building style popular in the 1920s and 1930s that often features bright colors and shapes.

chunk: A segment, or part, in the *Minecraft* world. One chunk is 16 blocks wide, 16 blocks long, and 256 blocks high.

complex: Having many parts.

explode: To suddenly release energy that causes harm.

gravity: The force that pulls objects toward Earth's center.

lever: A piece that is used to operate a machine.

mob: A moving creature within *Minecraft*. Often used to mean one of the monsters that spawns, or appears, in *Minecraft* at night.

mode: A form of something that is different from other forms of the same thing.

nugget: A bit of metal.

obstacle: Something that makes it difficult to complete an action.

resource: Something that can be used.

smelt: To heat to separate metals.

spawn: To bring forth. In video games, when characters

Index

A
activator rail, 19

B
blocks, 6, 10, 11,
      16, 20
brick, 10, 11

C
chests, 9, 12,
      18, 20
chunk, 7
coal, 6, 8
crafting table, 8
Creative mode, 6

D
detector rail, 18
diamond, 6

F
furnace, 8, 12, 14

G
gold, 6, 14
gravel, 11
gravity, 11, 20

H
hopper, 13

I
ingots, 8, 9, 14
iron, 6, 7, 8, 9

L
lava, 10, 11
lever, 14, 18

M
mob, 12, 16
mods, 22
monsters, 4,
      16, 18

O
ore, 6, 7, 8, 14

P
pickaxe, 6
powered rails,
      14, 17

R
rails, 6, 8, 9, 10,
      11, 12, 13,
      14, 16, 17,
      18
redstone, 14, 15,
      18, 19

S
sand, 10, 11
sandbox game,
      4, 5
ScriptCraft, 22
station, 16, 18, 20
sticks, 6, 8, 14
stone, 6, 8, 10, 11
Survival mode,
      4, 6

T
TNT, 12, 20
torches, 6, 14, 15

W
water, 10, 11
wood, 6, 8

Websites

Due to the changing nature of Internet links, PowerKids Press has developed
an online list of websites related to the subject of this book. This site is
updated regularly. Please use this link to access the list:
www.powerkidslinks.com/stemmc/railroads